To Judith & Herm —
To friends I rar[ely]
get to see but who
are always with m[e]
Love —
Ann

LOOKING BACK

Poems

by Ann Avery Andres

Contents

ACKNOWLEDGMENT

This book of poetry is dedicated to my husband, Gene, who has been more than supportive of all I've ever wanted to do and then some.

And to my two children Annalee and Charlie who are the two most precious gems in my jewel box of life.

And lastly, with fondest memories of endless hours of poetry to the Gypsy Scholars:

Jean Sanford

Bernice Chase

Carole F. Simson

Elizabeth Halsted

Margery Rendahl

PREFACE

These poems have been written over a period of about fifty years beginning with college and going through all the other stages of my life. Many were written while on vacation since then there was usually more time available for writing. The vacations reflected in the poems took place in Hong Kong, the Soloman Islands, Vanautu and Provence, France.

Several of the poems were written while on vacation at our beach house in San Clemente—long since sold.

In review, I see that the early poems are more dark in outlook. Perhaps that is because I was raised with the fear of mushroom clouds looming over me. Also, I was taken with existentialism while in college.

The dedication to The Gypsy Scholars are to the group of ladies with whom I studied literature and art at Oxford College one summer. We re-grouped every year thereafter for more than 20 years in Inverness, Northern California , studying a pre-selected poet. These poets included Dylan Thomas, Wallace Stevens, Seamus Heaney, T.S. Eliot, Walt Whitman, William Carlos Williams, Robert and Elizabeth Browning, Adrienne Rich, Shakespeare's Sonnets, W.H. Auden, W.B. Yeats, Denise Levertov, Emily Dickinson, Henry Wordsworth. The group stopped meeting when several members became too ill to travel and when our leader, Jean Sanford, died. I have many memories of our days together walking, admiring wild flowers and reciting and reading poetry.

I also received inspiration from my book club of over 14 years, The Green Parrot Literary Society. We have read and discussed over 172 books including a Victorian classic every December led by the Victorian literary scholar Andrea Gazzaniga.

Some of my poems were written specifically for certain people. Those very personal poems have not been included.

FOR NO KNOWN REASON

Out of nowhere, in front of our amazed eyes,
the tree just collapsed downward
taking with it its' twin
and smashing the fence inward over the creek.

For no known reason, sometimes, life collapses downward
and we are startled and wonder why.
The mystery is not explained by books nor theology
because in them questions are answered one way or another.

But, for no known reason, the tree came crashing down.

GROWING OLD

A snowy egret is not an usual sight in Santa Ana.
But one Sunday in April, we saw one flying low
over our back garden.

The black crows and green parrots were out shown
by this lone snowy egret whose magnificence lit up
the shadows of evening tide.

It swooped and flew low over the flower beds
ignoring us and all we own; we had no fish in the ponds then
to temp them into landing.

Egrets are rare guests among the usual squirrels,
crows, parrots and coyotes.
But they are welcome here in the glooming of old age,
reminding us of days past when beauty and grace
were a more common occurrence.

TORTURE

Torture and pain have always been off-limits;
it is unbearable to face unnecessary suffering.
Closing my eyes in movies, avoiding watching inflicted pain,
and torture scenes,
the reality of man's inhumanity to man
does not have to be pictured or explained to be real to me.

Perhaps subconsciously I must have suspected
that I would myself live with pain someday.
That day has come. Will it go?

Someone dear told me, "that which you fear the most
will happen but with God's help, you will cope."
Coping is an art—a state of mind,
an option I want to choose.
Can I? Will I? I need God's help.

RECOVERY

Crows swooping and soaring singly or
together around St. Josephs hospital--
the only signs of life seen from the windows of ICU.

Birds, Emily Dickinson's Hope,
become my hope, too.
The hope of all seeking recovery.

Hope that never really leaves us
but flutters quietly inside
or swoops and soars gracefully outside
in the morning's first light.

BOOKS REMEMBERED

Books filed away on library shelves once read
but now forgotten,
cry out to be remembered once again.
But which ones are so meaningful, relevant
as they once were to us?
Reflecting past interests, past conditional reactions,
these dusty books now stand solemn, sentient,
grim reminders of a youth, not so lost as forgotten—
lying latent within our aged memories.
Our beautiful literary jewels now stand silent, waiting
to be retouched
not by electronic connections but by human hands.

IMAGING

Suspended in a steal capsule, isolated in cold space,
a strange voice speaks in unidentifiable language.
Unrecognizable words, harsh staccato syllables
are the only sounds, the only connection to the outside world.
You wonder if it still exists.

Time is caught between the hands of minutes
which pass oh so slowly in the endless void.
The mind becomes muted in this utter suspension of stimuli
and the floating in space continues without pause
until you emerge once again in the world, on earth, in the clinic.
Finished with your M R I.

TO MY GRANDCHILDREN

We head to Calico Ghost Town early on a November day
all bundled together in the Land Rover.
Covering miles of sand and sage bush, the brown hills
rise up on our left.

Deep in the earth, we were told, minerals formed into
gold, silver and unfinished gems
nourished and sustained by mother earth
until discovered by known and unknown miners.
The gems are cut and polished into beautiful jewels and valuable
stones.
So, too, is the process of your lives.

From unformed molecules to human form,
shaped and polished by life's experiences, sadness's, joys,
interactions with family and friends and strangers.

You, my dearest ones, are discovered; have become the
most precious gems in my jewel box of life.

HIGHWAY 5

Traveling north from south, following Franciscan footsteps,
we transverse California's spine.
This spring,   poppies and lupin paint the grapevine hills
with spreading splotches of color and wild muster
tinges natural grasses a delicate light yellow.
Granville Redman has come to life before our gaze—
previously only a mirrored image but now face to face.

Down into the Central Valley we drop into long straight flatlands.
Quilt-like squares of nature's bounty shimmer in
the haze of sun-drenched air.
Fecund, earthy smells mingle with the acrid odor of cattle
held docile in vast pens awaiting their man-determined fate.

The car sways to the rhythm of the wind which is
always at home in the Pacheco Pass.
The reservoirs' waters shudder and wrinkle with gentle movement
besides the tamed and muted hills standing tranquilly by.

Unseen but known, the Pacific Coast follows us
just beyond the western hills—our silent companion.
To the east, the California aqueduct courses northern melted snows
southward at the cost of resentment and division of our unity.

A dusty tumbleweed crawls slowly along the edges of the fields
nudged by spurts of wind hurrying it along
until caught against the bard wire boundaries of its world.
We leave them stacked there, dried out and dusty,
small balls of western memories of when tumbleweeds
freely moved unfretted across our plains.

It is reported that Highway 5 can be seen from outer space—
specks of car lights stretching all in a line
down California valleys and over hills.
Are these restless souls searching for a new experience or
the same experience performed in another space?

Is this Highway then like the "California Dream"?
Moving, moving we think forward but maybe not.
At least this changing of scenery
brown to green and green to brown going up and down
refreshes the eyes; nourishes the soul with all its beauty.

A NIGHT AT THE OPERA

"L'Italiana en Algiri" Santa Fe, New Mexico

From the Santa Fe Opera House, we watch
turquoise and coral swirls color the Sangre Christos Mountains
like Southwestern jewelry.

We sip champagne as darker clouds roll in
slowly erasing color from the evening sky in patches of darkness.
Stravinsky stares from his bronze pedestal—
stern, saying nothing—

As darkness wraps a black, silk shawl around us,
all the colors go, except for the distant Los Alamos lights
blinking where science plays its own melodies.
The music of Rossini begins.

Algiri isn't any more ominous than this night in Santa Fe
where mysterious nuclear lights dance to the heavenly music.

FROM THE HOSPITAL WINDOW AT DAWN

Old, black crow hiding among the dark branches of the pine tree,
aligned with the fuzzy brown pine cones,
whose spiral points reach upward, upward.
Old, black crow your shadow unfolds briskly from the green shadows
to swoop and swing higher, lower--over to visit the neighboring elm.

Do you not see the opalescent clouds moving all alone above you,
dragging the lightest blue/grey wash of early morning sky behind?
Do you not see me—here through the window?
I hear your raucous cry, always coarse, cruel and unwanted.
But today even its disconsonance seems to have found a glorious
early morning
melody consistent with the unfolding of this brand new day.

CLOUDS OF BOKISSA

Over islands eternally green; over Pacific waters meters deep
float piles and piles of grey/white clouds
shrouding these island jewels and turning the emeralds
and the turquoises into slates and agates.

Preceding the darkness of the night sky, the grey period
of the day drags the daylight willingly into evening.
Colors fade as memory lingers on thoughts of you,
my daughter.

Winds through the leaves overhead play even songs
reminding us the Holy Ghost lives only twenty minutes away.
But you lie thousands of miles away on the land of the long white
cloud.
Will you break through this cloud cover before the millennium?
Will I ?

Evening darkens and quietly throws a dull blanket over all.
There is no longer cloud cover but darkness overhead.
We wait for you.

SYCAMORE CALENDAR 1987

Again…it's August and the Sycamores
arch high above the street forming a tunnel of sun-sucked leaves,
tan and rustling in the lanquid air.

I watch, have watched the seasons pass
reflected in each leaf's re-action to sunlight, moon beans or the rain.
In early summer, deep, green shadows overhead
relieve the street of sun bright heat
and make us want to walk beneath the silence of the leaves.

In fall, the leaves, fried brown, drop, crunch, blow
helplessly a swirl in the Santa Ana winds
leaving only dark stick figures reaching toward the sky.

Winter rains wet the branches, tear off hunks of skin.
Lonely black fingers appear before the moon and
mark its' passage as it travels across the night sky.

How sweet the buds of spring . Without effort, without a sound,
new leaves emerge in shades of green to dress the branches
in new clothes which shimmer and dance gaily
and whisper to us awesome blessings.

Each season the same; Sycamores marking off my life
in measurable increments like sands steadily,
irreversibly flowing downward in time's clock.

How long can this Sycamore calendar of life repeat itself so exactly?
How long will I cross off each numbered season?
Each season has its' glory
and I refuse to count.

SOLOMON SOLITUDE

Tambea Lagoon, visible through palm fans
and banana leaves,
moves ceaselessly in and out creating tropical wave music
soothing and re-distributing time upon
us and the greying shore.

Morning coolness welcomes early exploration
of deep canyon corals where
angels, manatees and sea snakes lurk and wait.
Unaware of our scrutiny, underwater life continues in endless motion,
in tune with unheard, unseen celestial undulations.

From our bungalow we listen to Pacific music played upon sea harps
and watch geckos bake on sun-drenched stones
among the lilies and sword ferns.
A single path leads the way out of paradise
and forward.

We will take this path a few days hence, but for now
we listen to the music
and move slowly among sea creatures.

SUMMER HOUSE IN PROVENCE

Vaison de la Romain

Summer 1995

Down the meadow, tree tops wink green and silver;
cigales sing among the leaves and re-act to the sun's strong heat
by ignoring us as we sit around our table in the shade.

Out the door, the earth is gray, turning dark here and there
where the court yard tree spreads out a blanket
of moving shadows for our summer comfort.

Beyond the court yard orchards and vineyards stand still;
their strength focused on silent reproduction.
Only the cherry tree shares her sweetness with us that summer.

Behind the setting sun, Mt. Ventoux comes in and out
of summer haze to look down on lessor but more jagged Dentelles
that hold our glaze in a tightening circle.

Neither the sun's rays nor summer's tears leave marks on chalky soil.
All are absorbed, traceless within minutes
of reaching the chalk white ground of Provence.

Within the town, detritus from Roman conquerors remind us
of how much civilization has been imposed and somehow absorbed
within the geography and architecture
but has not really changed this timeless place.

MAGGIE AND ME AND THE TREASURE HUNT

There's six children this summer at the beach.
Two are mine, two are friends and two are nieces—
children of my sister who is left behind this morning.

We start late but the tide is out and sea-treasures lay distributed,
waiting upon the smooth wet sand like odds and ends
scattered carelessly about on a glimmering vanity table.

Will our plastic bag hold all we want, all we snatch away
from the tides' ever closing fingers which
open in a moment of quick generosity but suddenly
close again, reclaiming treasures?

We move slowly along the shore, dark grey sand under foot.
Her prints barely mark the sand; mine are sharp-edged, deeper.
I want glass dulled by the seas repetitions and pock marked by sand.
She, her tastes not yet time-molded nor discriminate,
wants everything.

Into the bag go blue and red rocks (soon to turn black or brown on
the cottage porch) shells, seaweed, and bird feathers.
Her eyes are closer to the sand; she sees more.
She stoops over quickly like the sandpipers to snap up her finds.

For a long time, there's no one around to gage our progress,
question our selections. Then some joggers emerge from the distance.
We stand quite still, poised like startled deer.
They come upon us, quickly pass, too fast to notice all the
sea's largess.

We return to our morning treasure hunt finding
black butterflied mussels, perfect clan shells and worn down bits of glass.
Our bag is almost full.
Still we poke among the pools, touch sea moss and anemones with our toes.

It's time to end our treasure hunt. Sea treasures lose
their special charm when shared with too many, too much daylight.
Still, Maggie darts here and there picking up refuge or gold or a little bit of both?
With each find, she quite distinctly sing-songs "Thank you sea".

When we return, I wash off the treasures and Maggie
arranges them carefully on a round, plastic tray, bright yellow.
She shows them to the others as she walks through the room
stiffly, afraid the tray will slip and let them fall.

Each child selects a favorite, arguing a little over choices made.
But they don't look quite so rich on the plastic tray
as they had that morning on the wet, dark grey sand.

THE BEACH HOUSE

San Clemente

Through the window a skyline melts into ocean,
stretching horizontally to the picture's edge
and, in faith, beyond.
The subject never changes—just the colors
and the textures ebb and flow reflecting climatic whims
or the omnipresent rhythm of time unfolding day into day.

The murky blue-grey of dolphins' skin colors an early spring time morning.
Then the stabbing sparkle of sunlight leaps up from the sea to greet high noon
on a cloudless summer day in San Clemente.
A fuzzy tangerine sun highlights the monochrome slate grey of a winters evening
and lets streaks of yellow-orange seep across the horizon
before darkness draws the window closed
and you only know the view from memory and the sounds of waves.

The view has been the same from this beach house
since the early 1920s when Ole Hanson so carefully laid out his dream city
among the gorges and ravines leading down to the Pacific shore.
Only tonalities change within the seasons and within each day—
a gallery of tonalism paintings with subject tried and true.

Yet…it's the repetitiveness that fascinates, that comforts
that eternalizes time, bringing us here so regularly
to look eagerly out the window to make sure nothing has changed.

THE DAY AFTER THE FOURTH OF JULY
AT THE SAN JUAN HOT SPRINGS

1982

Sometimes there's a pause, a sudden slowing of the brain's calculations,
as if our life clocks skip beats letting us drop down in between
the hours—forgotten.

Like today going to the San Juan hot springs and enjoying
falling into the cracks of timelessness.
The wine, like the natural setting, tugs against
any inclination to push ahead.

So, we pause and start the process of absorbing this new environment,
man made by re -arranging nature's elements.
But only just a little.

We are surrounded by a thousand million shades of green leaves,
hung up overhead by oak, birch and California pine trees.
They leave a quiet blanket of silence broken only by our voices and the
sound of water.

The natural hot springs gurgle down in hidden pipes from
basins dug out long ago by Indians on the hillside up above.
What native medicine man foresaw the use of this his holy water?
More needed now, perhaps, than then.

We lean back against the sides of the wooden tubs
already grown slick to the touch
like the cool, green skin of wet frogs.

A bell jar silence lingers and enfolds us broken only by the sound
of air jets through the water leaving a wilted white foam--
the kind that edges ocean waves on a calm and very sultry day.

The water swirls and clings heated by a natural fire beneath the earth.
Too hot at first, painful on sun burned skin,
it soon becomes a thermal quilt down-like into which we snuggle.

Giving in to the undulations of water, sun and shade,
we slowly move backward through a maze of configurations
formed by each decision, non-decision made
until we regain, almost, an earlier time.

A king snake, easing slowly along the heated path, is a momentary diversion.
We admire its languid symmetry until it disappears among the birches.
My son sees it later, higher up on a branch. I'm not able to distinguish it
again among the greenery, yet I tell him I can see it.

Overhead, as if sprinkled from an old cut-glass sugar jar,
sunlight begins to filter through the trees.
It lays freckled upon your face thrown carelessly backward
against the wooden tub.

Unaware of my scrutiny, how unlined it looks today
matching my memories when I watched you
twenty years ago doze on an Hawaiian beach while I
wrote a term paper on Turgenev.

Slowly separating the layers of this tranquility
like a persistent worry, it comes to us that the clock's tick grows
loud as the shadows darkly lengthen.

We hear the ticking, feel the gravitational tug within and
know that time as been submerged—not drowned.
I wonder what you'll remember of this day—the day
after the fourth of July, of the pause between the hours,
of the clock that didn't stop, just paused to let us breathe.

MOTHER

She was less than a paragraph in the Jones history;
a very insignificant person in the world scheme of things
impacting history not so very much,
if at all.

But within myself I feel real loss and grief.
She is gone; there's no one there now to clot the flow
of my heart's blood out of me yet going no where.

The sense of loss is pushing aside other feelings
which once filled up the spaces, kept the equilibrium.
I am afloat, unbalanced without her love's anchor.
I am a tiny child again lost in the darkness.

ON THE BIRTH OF OUR SON
July 24, 1971

A joyous being's come to add
another budding branch
to our Tree of Life made glad
by a branch so little it can't find
the sun nor stars nor moon
without the help of its own kind.

But one day soon the branch will be
a support for many other things
like robin's nests and children's swings.

It will reach up to the sky when strong,
and bending with the gusty winds
make its own melodies, sing its own songs.

Yet nothing is as what it seems.
We're just a part of larger schemes.
Even so with branches bold.

For they extend on into time
from something larger than the tree
with their own legacies, their own histories
adding to our Tree of Life made glad
each and every time.

ON THE BIRTH OF OUR DAUGHTER

May 26, 1970

Lovely child of love's perfection,
yours the soft but sure reflection
of the souls of generations lost.

In rapturous joy you were conceived.
In awesome joy you were received
by us the nominees before.

And now you've come to add another
shiny, golden link to smother
pain from parted beings now remembered.

Sweetly smile child of endearment.
Mock the darkness of entombment
with your glowing presence real.

You are our love child come to render
us the beauty of sublime surrender
to the beat of life unending.

Lovely child of love's perfection,
yours the soft but sure reflection
of the souls of generations lost.

TIME, THE COMPANION OF MY YOUTH

My old Companion stopped for me and held her breath
to let me breathe.
With some impatience She waited there while we,
soul mates of a flickering hour,
greedily ate from the pro offered destined fate.

We tasted fruits known but then unknown as if awakening
from a numbing sleep.
And then, oh then we held the restless reigns and filled
the universe with our caress.
Defying man-made laws we spanned the seas
to warm to life the blood of a thousand buried hours.

We consumed the wine of ancestral bitter sweet,
with golden smiles and dancing feet.
No twilight time denied our sun-filled happiness.

Sea-hewed shells was your essence and your source;
wine-red my grand response.
And, I swear, never two souls with less remorse
nor two beings so rightly lost to the counter confessions
of a faceless clock.

Then, from across the grey of a sure awakening
to that last hour that runs astray, I heard my Companion calling me.
And, harkening to the solemn sound of reality
I danced away.

THE INNER ME WAITING TO EMERGE

Out of my soul flows forth sweet longings that
do not match the constant vehemence of my words,
words that disguise the inner me.
I am weak and have not the strength to fight the
preconditioned me seen only through what I do and what I say.

I sorrow for the smoke-like loveliness of inner profundity
which goes unnoticed as the nascent butterfly.
But I know it's poised and ready for a wondrous flight
if I can get beyond the preconditioned me.

I am saddened that the poetry of my soul goes unexpressed.
To be a poet. School, job, marriage, children cry out objections
to which I listen for the present.
But a Song-Of-Myself waits to be sung by my inner me
and soars about in uninhibited ecstasy and joy.
If only in my dreams.

THE GOOD BUTTERFLY

Purple orchids moist and warm crying their desire
while the butterfly soars higher ignoring the fire.
Landing lightly now on the sweet smelling flowers,
she catches her lithe wings on the ugly briers—
only once in awhile.

Piercing thorns hardly scaring the delicate wings,
only biting intricate designs on the swirling rings.
Now hopping onto a moon bean, absorbed in the light;
poor butterfly heading on to darkening night—
not yet in style.

WONDERING WHY

What strange forces direct our fate?
What hand shuts the door and turns the key?
Is man a victim of some wind or man a victim of mere man?

Can the rock be lifted from the shoulders
or must it remain where placed?
The rock grows heavy and the eyes look round and round
and stare into the heavy air.
Alas, the world seems barren and quite unfair
to one so strong yet so vulnerable there.

With so many questions eternally unanswered
one wonders at the human sacrifice
of carrying rocks at all.

RIGHTSIDE UP REALITY

Take me away from sounds that grieve,
from all the faceless faces.
I've heard too often, I've seen too much.
I've drunk deeply from the cup of bitter sweet.

I always said sometime I'd go, I'd go, I'd go.
But like a broken record, I kept repeating tiresome phrases
and went nowhere.
I have no place to go to escape this upside down reality

But now we've met. I know you'll understand
what is really up and what is really down
because you have been there and seen through the veil.

Take me away from sounds that grieve, from all the faceless faces;
away from transitory things, from illusive saneness
to right side up reality.

LOVE'S RULES

From the sea comes a tide of love.
Surely it reaches the exposed and waiting shore
to gently add grain to golden grain.
Moon-time, dragging tides by the hand,
causes the now satisfied beach to be rich and rightly gorged.

In quiet innocence, the shore accepts her lover's gifts
and lounges in blissful unawareness
that across the sprawling span of water
her other side is ravenously attacked by the self-same tide of love
coming from the vast and moving sea.

Eating ugly crags and leaving scars,
this tide of love satisfies its eternal hunger
while giving generously to other shores, other lovers.
Beware of love's rules.

SEPARATION

Rendered sponge-like I was lying sunbaked
and staring at the sun.
Shouldn't sponges know that water, not sun, is their salvation?

Flooding over me like an ocean tide you came
slowly, surely, growing, crashing.
And I, only in submergence breathing
soaked you up and welcomed saturation.

Tugged by worldly forces, you receded
for not even ocean tides are always free to move at will.
The hypnotic sun was left to rule
a dried out shell, void of life-giving substance.

Ah, sea gulls —unmindful of the rules
fly freely toward the West.
But I can't even breathe.

YOUNG LOVE

Because love is transitory, lingering only for an instant,
I must touch you, I must make you know me.
Don't hesitate—accept the lovely knowledge
that only for a moment does the universe stand still
and jealously offer us precious moments.
Don't lament—take it greedily and rejoice
for most aren't blessed with even an instant
and are blinded by the illusion of endless time.
Don't fight—surrender to the awful certainty of a passing hour,
to a clock that ruthlessly drags separation by the hand.

Be quick our hearts for it is oh so very sad.

A DEATH ON NEW YEAR'S EVE

Now and once again, Time ascending catches man in a suspended hour—
sprawls him upon a faceless clock to stand witness
before the final triumph of his mortality.
Such was the hour we gather all together in the half tones of the night.

Sounds of Death's shadow, audible and mournful linger on the air.
And, poised for news inevitable,   listening for the call to break
unmentioned sorrow into mourning, we wait each to each.

Mist huddling around the house, sealing in the sounds and shadows,
rolling thoughts into the tightest balls, alienates the real from the unreal.
Which is which?

So, curtained against the gayest eve of all, Death's whisperings
mute the sounds of the yearly celebration
as we listen to the heavy air, listen to the chorus of exploding
fiery salutations.

Each to each; each to none; none to one.
With questions caught between being and being gone,
a wordless void emerges.
And the ever present shadow of finite life moves among us.
Then, surely as the melting mists, surely as the fading glory
of another yearly birth, the shadow of an old man leaving
passes across the room and mingles with the night.

THE BEAUTIFUL UPSIDE DOWN CAKE

This is the story of the beautiful upside down cake.
Profoundly beautiful because she doesn't know she's upside down.
For her, upside down is right-side up and right-side up is upside down.

My how she's been turned around.

But lucky me. I know her mistake because I'm the one who's right-side up.
Yes. I'm definitely right-side up because…well because everybody tells me so.
I'm right-side up just like they are and all the peoples always have been
(except when they were being born). I'm so glad I'm right-side up
so that I can put the confused upside down cake straight.

But silly upside down cake. Doesn't even know
she's downside up and upside down.

My how she's been turned around!

NOCTURNAL ENCHANTMENT

Snuggled down in fluffy white,
curled into a ball of dreams,
lost among the folds of night,
stealing stars and silver beams.

Sneaking in on stocking feet
with a tiptoe and a sigh
comes the dream child sprinkling sleep
making moments whisper by.

Visions pass in fantasy,
a parade of tones and hues.
Mystic myriads do I see
all in violets, greens and blues.

Star by star dreams flicker out
as blazing sun announces day.
Waking doubt has come to stay
and all sweet dreams have faded 'way.

A TWENTIETH CENTURY EDUCATION

Ah, Men of Reason, of Absolute Truth.
You are long last dead.
They have slaughtered you!
The bells toll while the pavement slips
under our indeterminate world.
We reach out for balance.
Our empty hands grasp subjectivity and transitory metaphysics.
We walk in an existential dilemma.

We look around at the beautifully substantial city.
Yet not so substantial but that our dreams
awoke in a mushroom cloud.
We are told that our reality was but a hope, an admirable aspiration
of minds confused and wishful thinking.

Ah, for blissful unawareness, for days of seeing , knowing ignorance.
For times of touching the illusion and feeling there solid comfort;
for words of absolutes, words of standards.
But we've outgrown such need for total cognition
or so we are taught.

We've escaped all this knowing and this careful understanding
of what is right and what is wrong, what is real and what is false.
We hope for Truth but the Truth we are taught haunts us until we turn
to see her face to face…and go blind.

LEARNING TO LIVE WITH THE ATOMIC BOMB

1963

Birds in flight.
Shadows flickering.
Time is told in moments only.

I wait expectantly
with eager hopes
only to hear the cry
of disappearing birds
and of man.

Biography

ANN AVERY ANDRES was born and raised in Long Beach, California in a family compound and was surrounded by family. She attended the University of Redlands and then UCLA from which she was graduated. She became a high school teacher and taught English in Japan while her husband, Eugen, was stationed in Yokosuka. She was the first American to receive a Japanese teaching credential. Ann also taught English and history in high schools in Long Beach.

After moving to Santa Ana, California, Ann earn a J.D. degree in law and has
for the past 35 years practiced with her husband. They have two grown children and five growing grandchildren.

Beginning with a college course in creative writing, Ann has been writing poetry. "Looking Back…" is a collection of her poems over 50 years.

Made in the USA
Charleston, SC
02 July 2015